YOUR KNOWLEDGE HAS VALUE

Ruhaim Izmeth

Employee Tardiness and Working Conditions in Burgers Hut

GRIN Publishing

Bibliographic information published by the German National Library:

The German National Library lists this publication in the National Bibliography; detailed bibliographic data are available on the Internet at http://dnb.dnb.de .

Imprint:

Copyright © 2013 GRIN Verlag GmbH
Print and binding: Books on Demand GmbH, Norderstedt Germany
ISBN: 978-3-656-85873-7

This book at GRIN:

http://www.grin.com/en/e-book/285101/employee-tardiness-and-working-conditions-in-burgers-hut

GRIN - Your knowledge has value

Since its foundation in 1998, GRIN has specialized in publishing academic texts by students, college teachers and other academics as e-book and printed book. The website www.grin.com is an ideal platform for presenting term papers, final papers, scientific essays, dissertations and specialist books.

Visit us on the internet:

http://www.grin.com/

http://www.facebook.com/grincom

http://www.twitter.com/grin_com

Employee Tardiness and Working Conditions in Burger's Hut

by Ruhaim Izmeth - Submitted on Aug - 2013 to BMS

Abstract / Executive Summary

This case study investigated the work-environment related reasons behind employee tardiness in a recently established fast food joint, 'Burger's Hut'. It was found, after observation sessions and interviews that late night work shifts and non-flexible leave scheduling were the main reasons for the problem. It is recommended that the Burger's Hut develops a strict policy to prevent tardy employees before the problem lead to other withdrawal behaviors like absenteeism and turnover.

Introduction / Rationale

Burger's Hut is a small fast-food outlet located in the heart of Dehiwala. Since its inception on December 2012, it has been popular for serving an unmatched menu and quality food at an affordable price, hence its slogan "Goodness in Every Bite".

A team of 9, most of whom have worked on a similar setting before, help operate the business daily from 1pm to 12 midnight on a shift basis. Recently, it's proprietor has noticed that tardy behavior of few employees has caused work disorientation leading to customer dissatisfaction and eventually loss of revenue.

There could be several reasons that cause tardiness. Since all of them could not be covered in a single research, it was decided to focus upon a subset of reasons that the management could address and rectify. The working conditions of employees are very much under the control of the management. Hence the purpose of the research became to investigate which work conditions if any that caused tardiness in the organisation.

The researcher will attempt to observe and speak to the employees of Burger's Hut to determine why they report late to work. By combining the research results of previous studies and the findings of this research the researcher makes recommendations to the Burger's Hut management on how to control the tardiness problem.

As this research only focuses on a small fast food outlet most of the findings will be more specific to the organisation. We will need more research on other similar outlets in the same industry to draw a generalized idea of the findings.

Problem statement

Which working conditions in Burgers Hut affect the tardiness of its employees?

Objectives

- To identify the factors that affect overall employee tardiness.
- To determine the working conditions that affect tardiness of employees in Burgers Hut.
- To provide recommendations to Burgers Hut on how to control tardiness.

Literature Review

Evolution of Human Food Consumption

The survival of early human settlements depended upon the ability to produce food to meet the need of the growing population. Most ancient civilizations like the Mesopotamians and Aztecs founded their settlements in the banks of great rivers like the Nile and Amazon. The availability of river water made the food production easier thus enabled the settlements to grow into great civilizations.

Global food consumption patterns have changed dramatically in recent years (Naska, 2006). One prominent trend has been the increasing consumption of fast food (Kearney, 2010). The fast food industry, originally conceived in Southern California during the 1940s, not only altered the eating habits of Americans, but also those in many other countries around the world, including Sri Lanka (Schlosser, 2001).

The boom of the Fast Food Industry

In the US alone, the fast food industry accounted to 190 billion in sales for the year 2012 and employs a workforce of over 4.6 million in close to 300,000 establishments (NAICS , 2013). Big players like the McDonalds and KFC are flourishing by catering to this growing demand (Kalman, 2012). The growth of McDonald's in US is highlighted concisely by Schlosser in his literature, Fast Food Nation (2001) ,

> "The McDonald's Corporation has become a powerful symbol of America's service economy, which is now responsible for 90 per cent of the country's new jobs. In 1968, McDonald's operated about one thousand restaurants. Today it has about thirty thousand restaurants worldwide and opens almost two thousand new ones each year. An estimated one out of every eight workers in the United States has at some point been employed by McDonald's. The company annually hires about one million people, more than any other American organization, public or private."

In Sri Lanka, KFC began operations in the year 1995 and has grown to operate 24 outlets in 2013 (Cargills (Ceylon) PLC : KFC, 2013). McDonalds already operates 6 outlets in Colombo and its suburbs.

New entrants, like the Burgers Hut, have to overcome a lot of challenges to be competitive with the big names (Avermaete et al., 2003). Consumers' food purchase intentions are based on factors such as safety, freshness, storage, preparation, consumption, price, packaging, and place of purchase.(Grunert, 2005; Röhr et al., 2005). Fast food companies attempt valiantly to strike a balance between these factors to deliver the best product at the best price.

Labour sourcing in the Fast Food industry
The rate of growth of the fast food industry has opened up a huge demand for human labour. Statistics in the US indicate an average of 16-17 workers per fast food establishment (NAICS , 2013). Two of the major HR problems faced by the fast food multinationals(MNC) are a) sourcing cheap labour and b) high turnover (Royle, 2002).

Royle (2002) also reports a few ways the MNCs use to overcome the above problems. The tasks carried out by a fast food worker is Taylorised, or broken down into simplified, routine and systematic jobs of production in which the workers are allocated to specialize in. Taylorism allows low/unskilled labour to be hired and get the new hires up to speed with little or no training. It also eases in finding replacement after a worker leaves the organisation.

Fast food work is one of the least paid jobs in the US and has no viable career progression path to the worker (Schlosser, 2001). Statistics show that many workers quit 6 months into the job and most before a year. Knowing this, the MNCs prefer hiring young adults. A study in 1994 showed that nearly 70% of fast food workers were 20 years or older(Van Giezen, 1994). Workers in this age category have low wage expectations and no long term plan to be in the industry. The MNCs target this group in their CSR projects to attract and source their future employees.

Challenges faced by Fast Food employees
Though might be fair in the MNC perspective, the rights of the actual worker is often overlooked or if brought to the limelight, quickly silenced by the MNC itself(Drapp, 1998; Colton, 1998; Bernstein, 1998). Most grievances raised by the fast food workers are understaffed shifts, unpredictable schedules, late night work, wage inequalities, routinized work and tyrannical supervision (Royle, 2002).

Routinization has made fast-food work be considered unskilled labour, on the contrary, to perform well it requires dexterity, endurance and capacity to keep many things mind at once, particularly to those who serve food and interact with the customers. There is substantial 'emotional labour' involved during busy periods which makes work hard and exhausting (Leidner,1993).

A common complaint made by fast food workers is that scheduling of work times and time off is unfair and unpredictable. The situation aggravates when the worker is asked to skip his/her time off because of peak season or to make up for an unplanned absence.

"Off-the-clock work" is another problem faced by fast food workers (Tannock, 2001), ie. many workers perform labour, often in small segments of time, for which they are not paid. For example, working through their break times, 'helping out' co-workers before or after their own shifts or doing cleanup work after a shift ends.

Most fast food outlets including Burgers Hut operate till late night and requires the crew to be functional throughout this period. Night work makes it mandatory for the subjects to stay awake and to perform duties, when their body is physiologically programmed to remain asleep (Horowitz and Tanigawa, 2002). It also retards performance, elevates occupational stress and tiredness thus leading to deteriorating quality in family and social life (Fujino et al. 2001; Pati & Chandrawanshi 2001; Suzuki et al. 2004)

Employee Tardiness

Employee Tardiness can be described as arriving late to work or leaving before the end of the shift (Shafritz, 1980). It is a problem found in many organizations. It has implications for the employee as well as for the organization as a whole. (Dishon-Berkovits, M, & Koslowsky, M 2002).

Tardiness seems to be a less researched topic. Analysing organizational behavior literature between 1990-92 (Blau, Linnehan, Brooks & Hoover,1993) revealed 23 studies of turnover,13 of absenteeism, and none of tardiness. For this reason researcher believes that researching more on this will enable to derive new knowledge and validate previous research.

Effects of Tardiness

Employee tardiness leads to substantial financial costs (Blau, 1994; Steers & Rhodes, 1984). It causes loss of productivity of the late employee and loss of productivity of fellow workers(Groeneveld & Shain, 1985). When working to make up for their co workers who are late the fellow workers experience a deterioration of their morale and work motivation (Cascio, 1987; Jamal, 1984).

Most researchers have seen tardiness as an aspect of withdrawal behavior (Hanisch & Hulin, 1990). They see tardiness as correlated with absenteeism which ultimately paves way to employee turnover. Also a tardy employee's behavior may be viewed as negligence (disrespect) toward the organization
and its values (Bolin & Heatherley, 2001)

Employers may or may not record late arrival in personal files of employees. Absences, on the other hand, is generally recorded in an individual's file. Additionally, lateness can often be made up on the
same day, and, therefore, not regarded as a less serious violation of organizational rules.(Dalton & Todor, 1982; Koslowsky, 1987).

However, Clegg (1983), Johns & Nicholson (1982) and Nicholson (1977) explain that tardiness should not be seen only as a predictor of withdrawal behavior or as an instance of job dissatisfaction. An employee arriving late to work does not necessarily mean that he is dissatisfied with the job or has plans to leave the organization soon.

Factors affecting Tardiness

Researchers with varied perspectives have introduced new variables that impact tardiness. One explains it with economic models; tardiness as a function of the interplay between time resources allocated to work and leisure (Allen, 1981; Leigh & Lust, 1988).

Work–family conflict is another cause of tardiness , especially for women and for younger couples (Blau, 1994; Gupta & Jenkins, 1983). Weather conditions (Muesser, 1953), health concerns and transportation problems have also been found to cause tardiness.

According to an article published on CNN.com by CareerBuilder, responses given by employees for question 'What are the biggest causes of their tardiness?' are, twenty-seven percent of workers blamed traffic; 10 percent pointed to getting their kids ready for school or day care; and 11 percent said falling back asleep. Another interesting statistic revealed was that 64 percent of employers said Monday was the most popular day for late arrivals.

A research done with female telephone operators (Adler & Golan, 1981) show that job dissatisfaction and work stress were generally significant predictors of lateness. Angle & Perry, (1981) show that low commitment of employee to organization leads to a high tardiness rate with bus drivers. Being unmindful of his or her personal development and achievements also lead to employee tardiness behavior (Shapira & Griffith, 1990).

One strand of relevant literature is found in the analysis of transportation choice and urban traffic congestion. Here, the focus is not on lateness per se but rather on the scheduling of (typically commuting) trips. A key explanatory variable, in addition to the explicit cost of transport mode and journey time, turns out to be the degree of flexibility in arrival time enjoyed by the employee. Abkowitz (1981), Caplice and Mahmassani (1992) and Small (1982) find that employer flexibility is a statistically significant determinant of scheduling decisions taken by urban commuters in American cities. This is consistent with the emphasis on monitoring and sanctions in the economic approach.

Job related aspects such as routinization (degree to which employee's jobs are repetitive); job hazards (degree to which employees are exposed to harmful working condition) and word overload more likely cause the employees to be tardy, leave work early and be absent (Allen, 1981; Brooke & Price, 1989; Ervin & Iverson, 1994; Johns, 1997; Price & Mueller, 1986). Conversely greater the coworker support, distributive justice (treating all employees fairly) and job satisfaction make employees less likely to express withdrawal behavior (Brooke & Price, 1989; Iverson et al.,1998; Koslowsky et al., 1997).

Environment variables like availability of alternative jobs outside the organization, external responsibilities (having responsibilities outside of work) and absence permissiveness (degree to which tardism and absenteeism is tolerated by the organisation) have also been associated with withdrawal behavior (Blau, 1994; Brooke & Price, 1989; Erwin & Iverson, 1994).

A study on 55 student nurses revealed that night work gives rise to lack of concentration, interest, energy, sleep and appetite (Adeniran et al. 1996). All the above researched characteristics builds a perfect profile of a fast-food worker, and will be interesting note the if the results of the research holds true for the fast food industry as well.

Researchers (Dishon-Berkovits & Koslowsky, 2002) on a study on factors determining punctuality, showed that employees who are impatient, easily aroused, angry and hostile tend to be punctual to work. A variable named "Time Urgency" was introduced in the study(Dishon-Berkovits & Koslowsky 2002) with a scale described by (Landy et al., 1991). This scale measured 33 items contributing to personality traits like the "speed of eating", "pace of talking" and "loudness of speech".Research found that the time urgency variable contributed positively to punctuality. Another interesting finding of the same research was that the, age of the youngest child of the employee also seemed to negatively contribute to tardiness (Dishon-Berkovits & Koslowsky, 2002).

A more recent research (Clark, Peters & Tomlinson, 2005) carried out on British workers defines 5 variables that contribute to tardiness -(i)Worker characteristics(gender,age, education, etc.), (ii) Workplace characteristics (public sector, private sector, unions), (iii)Sanctions and monitoring (dismissal policy on late comers, clocking of arrival and departure times), (iv)Incentives (extra payment for punctual attendance) and (v)Worker attitudes (job satisfaction). It found that lateness is higher for males, private sector workers and in service industries.

Determining the degree of Tardiness

Blau (1994) puts lateness behavior into 3 categories based on the frequency of occurrence and the lateness duration,

> (i) Increasing Chronic - characterized by a non random pattern of increasing frequency and duration, reasons for such behavior could be due to low job satisfaction,job involvement,organizational commitment

> (ii) Stable periodic - characterized by a non random pattern of stable frequency and duration, reasons for such behavior could be due to leisure, tradeoff and work-family conflict.

> (iii) Unavoidable - characterized by a random pattern of random frequency and duration, reasons for such behavior could be due to bad weather, transportation or accident

It is understood that there is no clear cut set of factors that influence tardiness in the workplace. An attempt to list out all such factors in a single research is not practical as there are large amounts of variables and interdepencies weaving them together.

Blau. G (1994) lateness behavior categorization allows researcher to determine the reasons for the tardiness problem Burgers Hut is facing, while the research approach defined by Clark, Peters & Tomlinson (2005) provide a systematic framework to apply these antecedents to find out its relationship with tardiness.

Methodology

Burgers Hut only employs 9 full-time workers, because of this the sample available was too small for a survey based research with quantitative analysis. The outlet has been open for almost a year and tardiness hadn't been recorded by the management throughout this period. Hence, there is very less solid data available for a descriptive research. Due to the less number in the sample and lack of detailed historical data, the researcher approaches this as an exploratory case study to analyse the problem qualitatively.

Since a solid cause for the tardiness trend had not been identified and as there could be several causes for this trend, this study was a correlational study and not causal one. The study was carried out in the natural setting (non-contrived) and minimal / if at all no interference was made by the researcher throughout the field study. Before interviewing employees, the researcher carried out non-participatory observation sessions in the guise of a customer who needs to purchase burgers. This allowed the researcher to make notes on the employee behaviors relating to the degree of enthusiasm the employees showed towards their jobs. Least interference caused the employees to exhibit their most natural behavior and not alter their behavior knowing that they are being watched.

It would be impractical to attempt to study this in a contrived environment as it would involve attempting to control variables which have not yet been identified. A contrived research should be possible after this study, as certain variables related to tardiness will be uncovered and could be controlled in further research.

All members of staff in the outlet were interviewed by posing to each one a set of structured open ended questions relating to tardiness, work environment, job satisfaction and pay. Interviews were conducted during the off peak hours of business and took no longer than 15 minutes. The off peak hours and time cap were deliberately chosen so that interviewees will be responding to questions more eagerly as they will be assured that their work will be the minimally interrupted. During the interview, the researcher explained the interviewees the purpose of the interview and assured them that their opinions will be handled confidentially. As open-ended questions could have long answers and noting every statement on paper could break the flow of the interview, the interviews were recorded via a dictaphone with the consent of the interviewee. The researcher wrote down to the greatest level possible, the responses of interviewees who did not consent the digital recordings.

The unit of analysis was individual as the focus of the study is to find out the reasons the individuals report to work late. The employees were only interviewed once during the study hence it was cross sectional analysis that took place. A longitudinal analysis will involve follow-up and will require constant monitoring over a longer period of time. Longitudinal analysis is best for a field experiment and not a field study, which allows the researcher to test by changing conditions or variables as needed. Given the time restrictions and the scope of the project the most relevant approach for this study was cross-sectional.

Since only a handful of employees were involved the researcher decided to include all individuals in the study. Though not all them were tardy, the researcher was interested in speaking to the non-tardy individuals to gain certain insights on the conditions that make them

7

not tardy.

Findings and Analysis

To analyse the tardiness trends the researcher spoke to the management to obtain past records of the clocking times of the employees. It was found that only absence records were maintained and clocking times were not being recorded. But the management reported that the trend of tardiness has been on the increase for the past few months. The researcher obtained the absence records to analyse if this trend has been the same for absence as well. This case confirms the findings of Dalton & Todor (1982) that most organisations overlook the recording of clocking data.

The researcher could not detect an increasing trend in the absenteeism patterns for the previous months. If increasing tardiness is seen as a withdrawal behavior in this instance, according to Hanisch & Hulin (1990), it should indicate an increasing absenteeism pattern as well. This was not true in the case of Burgers Hut. So researcher sees it safe to conclude that the tardiness behavior of Burgers Hut employees is not due to the cause of job dissatisfaction which most often should result in increasing absenteeism and later turnover.

For observational study, the researcher visited the outlet in 4 different days during different operation hours in guise of a customer who wanted to dine in. The researcher preferred to dine in because it provided a greater duration of observation than take away. On 2 occasions when the outlet was visited during the peak hours all dine-in slots were taken and the researcher had to content himself with a take away.

On all occasions the service was quick, the average serving time from the time of order was less than 3 minutes. The crew was very quick to respond to orders and were very enthusiastic on serving the customer. Though the researcher did not notice any sign of lethargy or wariness in the crew during the peak hours, signs of it were eminent during after off-peak times. This could be considered normal and not as a sign of job dissatisfaction.

Another advantage the researcher had by carrying out observation sessions was that it allowed the crew to get to know the researcher as regular customer and not as a researcher. This build up of researcher-crew relationship helped during the interview sessions, as the crew seemed more comfortable answering questions by a person whom they had seen and interacted with several times than answering questions by a total stranger.

The researcher managed to speak to all the employees except one. He refused to take part in the interview citing that he had difficulty in speech. This was confirmed by the management and the fellow workers.

The interview consisted of 8 structured open ended questions relating to work conditions and tardiness. When asked about pay, all employees were satisfied with what they were getting. Some had just had a pay rise and some had been promised one soon. In response to another question posed about how they would feel if they lost their jobs, most went on to say that even though they might find employment easily if they lost their jobs, it would be difficult to find one

8

that would match the pay at Burger's Hut.

Two workers were doubtful if they would look for a job in the same industry if they lost this job, instead would look for some independent source of income, like becoming a 3 wheel driver. They also emphasized that they felt that there was no career growth or enhancement if they continued to be in the fast food industry. In addition they complained about the work being too routinized, ie. you are to to the same work repetitively. This sometimes made their jobs boring as they did not learn or experience anything new apart from the routinized work. This also confirms Leidner (1993)'s findings.

The researcher also questioned about the future plans of the employees, amazingly, most saw themselves still working at Burger's Hut even 5 years down the line. When asked the reason, they said they were excited about the future of the outlet, because new menus were to be introduced and opening of a newer branch was in the talks. They feel that if the business goes well they too will also be treated well. An employee was interested in exploring the gem trade with one of his cousins, and another was saving up to purchase a 3 wheeler and give it out on rent. But both of them preferred to continue to work in Burgers Hut even after reached the said goals. Another worker said that he would leave Burger's Hut if he was selected for a job in the Middle East.

When asked about rest - all interviewees agreed that they did not have enough rest and that work times were difficult to orient to. On the duration of sleep they experienced, many of them had split their sleep to 2 or more sessions. Most, except one said that they fell asleep as soon as they got home from work, and slept until noon. But their sleep was usually interrupted for the pre-dawn prayer, breakfast, noisy children and running household errands.

All of them said that they didn't like their sleep being interrupted and had trouble going back to sleep after such interrupts. In addition all of them agreed that during periods of being awake between interrupts their bodies were not in 100% active mode. This finding also validates the study carried out by Pati & Chandrawanshi (2001) on how night work retards performance and deteriorates the quality of family and social live of the worker.

Another concern reported by some employees was the lack of flexibility in getting time off. According to Burger's Hut policy every employee is entitled to 1 day off per week. Employees are allowed to select the day of the week they wish to take leave, but management decides to approve it or not. If 2 or more employees request leave on the same day the leave is often not approved. If an employee needs to change the day of leave for any reason the management has to do a lot of rescheduling most often at the expense of a scheduled leave of one or more other employees. Some employees work leave-less for few weeks to get many consecutive days off which again requires a lot of rescheduling. This unpredictability often caused difficulty for married employees who felt that they could not properly attend to the needs of their spouses and children.

When asked the reasons for being tardy, a few reasons mentioned were transportation problems, lack of sleep or some medical condition like headache or body ache. Interestingly most employees didn't mind being tardy. Most of them thought that their tardiness will not cause a deficiency in operations. They were certain that another employee would cover up for it until the late employee arrives. Another reason they cited was that most sales during a shift happens in the peak hours (5-9pm) of the day and felt that they did not see a pressing need for them to be in time (3pm), which they considered early.

Though some employees were punctual, their work too had been disturbed because they needed to make up a for the few employees who are always late. All employees had to report to work in time to set up the outlet and prepare the place and be ready for business for the day. Tardy employees tend to skip this regularly because they are late. This has forced punctual employees to do the work of an additional person while preparing the outlet for business. Employees also need to do cleanup work at the end of shifts, which sometimes ends after standard shift timings. This makes punctual employees work more hours than the shift they are allocated to.As Tannoock (2001) explains the problem of "Off the clock work" also seem to the aftect Burger's Hut employees.

Conclusion

By speaking to both tardy and punctual employees the researcher managed to get a complete view of how tardiness was affecting the organisation. Though the researcher uncovered several reasons that made employees of Burger's Hut tardy, the purpose of this study was to identify only the work environment related reasons.

Overall the Burger's Hut employees seem to be stressed and overworked hinting that late night shift timings and non-flexible leave scheduling may be the cause for the tardy behavior. As many researchers (Hanisch & Hulin, 1990) cite that regular tardy behavior could lead to absenteeism and turnover, this trend was not observed the outlet.

Absenteeism trends did not seem to have been influenced by the growing tardiness trend as reported by the management. One reason for this, as the researcher sees, could be because the management strictly regulates the leave / absence system and employees are aware that their leaves are being recorded. Employees are aware that any attempt to be absent from work regularly will be more highlighted than getting late to work.

Another reason for employees to get late and get absent could be the pay. The study found that the employees were extremely happy with their pay which seems to be above the average market rate. Absent days are taken into consideration when the monthly salary is being calculated, getting absent will negatively impact the monthly salary the employee draws.

Though the researcher managed to uncover important reasons that caused tardiness, the approach used to determine them did have limitations. There would have been bias in employee responses obtained during the interview, though they were assured of confidentiality, there might have been other reasons that might have been exposed in the interview. As the interview only lasted a few minutes, that time is difficult to express or grasp every reason that could be the cause for the problem.

Since the same set of questions were asked from every employee, it could have been that an employee who completed his interview influenced the others to respond to the questions in a pre-planned way. During observation sessions the researcher only managed to a observe employees who were serving the customers, the employees working in the kitchen were not visible for observation.

Recommendations

Burger's Hut should not take its tardiness problem lightly. If the same trend continues it could create internal friction between punctual employees and the management and if not addressed promptly might result in employees leaving the organisation.

The researcher has a few recommendations for the Burgers Hut management to control the problem. Firstly it needs to start recording clocking times of the employees and make the employees aware about it. Availability of historical records will allow the management take decisions and back it up with evidence. If an employee needs to be laid off for tardiness, these records should act as proof against the him.

Secondly Burger's Hut needs to put in place a strict policy for tardiness, where there are verbal and written warnings are issued to regular late comers. Since most employees seem very loyal to the organisation laying them off on multiple counts of tardy behavior could be too costly but a warning could be accompanied by a monetary value deducted from the employees monthly salary.

As a proactive measure the management could offer an extra monetary bonus for employees who maintained punctuality throughout a specified period. This too should be wisely used. If the bonus awarded was too high and every employee becomes eligible to it, then the bonuses will eat into the overall profits earned.

It will also be effective if the management had meetings everyday or every other day at the beginning of shift timings. This will encourage employees to report to work in time because they need to participate in the meeting.

The management will also need to rethink its leave assignment policy. To prevent employees taking several consecutive days off, the management will need to enforce a maximum limit for the number of days that an employee could be in leave consecutively and the number of days an employee could work without being on leave. It is best to have a white board hung in a place visible to all employees indicating the leave schedule for a week. This will allow employees to take calculated decisions on the days they need to be off.

The management could also implement job rotation, where employees are constantly assigned to work in several areas of the outlet. This will prevent boredom due to routinization and allow employees to learn new skills and understand their strengths.

Limitations and Further Research

Further research is necessary to determine the degree of impact the late night shift timings and non-flexible leave scheduling have on the organisation. The proposed recommendations could be implemented and a longitudinal study could be carried out where data is collected and analysed periodically. This will allow to monitor the impact of implementing the recommendations.

As this research only focuses on a small fast food outlet most of the findings will be more specific to the the organisation. We will need more research on other similar outlets to draw a generalized idea of the findings.

References

Adeniran R, Healy D, Sharp H, Williams JM, Minors D, Waterhouse JM. 1996. Interpersonal sensitivity predicts depressive symptom response to the circadian rhythm disruption of nightwork. Psychol Med. 26:1211–1221.

Adler, S, & Golan, J 1981, 'Lateness as a Withdrawal Behavior', Journal Of Applied Psychology, 66, 5, pp. 544-554.

Allen, S. G. (1981). An empirical model of work attendance. Review of Economics and Statistics, 63,83–94.

Angle, H, & Perry, J 1981, 'An Empirical Assessment of Organizational Commitment and Organizational Effectiveness', Administrative Science Quarterly, 26, 1, pp. 1-14,

Avermaete, T., Viaene, J., Morgan, E. J., Crawford, N. (2003). Determinants of innovation in small food firms. European Journal of Innovation Management, 6(1), 8-17.

Bardsley, J, & Rhodes, S 1996, 'USING THE STEERS-RHODES (1984) FRAMEWORK TO IDENTIFY CORRELATES OF EMPLOYEE LATENESS', Journal Of Business & Psychology, 10, 3, pp. 351-365,

Bernstein, A. (1998) 'Striking while the griddle is hot', Business Week , 4 May: 6.

Blau, G. (1994). Developing and testing a taxonomy of lateness behavior.Journal of Applied Psychology, 79(6), 959–970.

Bolin, A., & Heatherley, L. (2001). Predictors of employee deviance: The relationship between bad attitudes and bad behavior. Journal of Business and Psychology

Blau, Linneban. P Brooks. A & Hoover ,D.1993. Vocational behavior 1990-1992: Personnel practices, organizational behavior, workplace justice, and industrial/ organizational measurement issues .Journal of Vocational Behavior, 43:133-197

Brooke, P. P., & Price, J. L. (1989), The determinants of employee absenteeism: An empirical test of a causal model, Journal of occupational Psychology

Cargills (Ceylon) PLC : KFC - Kentucky Fried Chicken . 2013.   Cargills (Ceylon) PLC : KFC - Kentucky Fried Chicken . [ONLINE] Available at: http://www.cargillsceylon.com/OurBusinesses/KFC.aspx. [Accessed 09 August 2013].

Cascio, W. (1987).Costing human resources: The financial impact of behavior in organizations(2nd ed.). Boston: Kent.

Castillo-Duran C, Castillo MA, Jackson P, Romo MM. Junk food consumption and child nutrition. Nutritional anthropological analysis. (cited 2006 Dec 30) PubMed 2004 Oct;132(10):1235-42.

Clark, K, Peters, S, & Tomlinson, M 2005, 'THE DETERMINANTS OF LATENESS: EVIDENCE FROM BRITISH WORKERS', Scottish Journal Of Political Economy, 52, 2, pp. 282-304

Colton, M. (1998) 'Big Mac attack: did somebody say strike? The kids who took on McDonald's—and won', Washington Post , 26 April: F1.

Dalton, D.R., & Todor, W.D. (1982). Turnover: A lucrative hard dollar phenomenon. Academy of Management Review

Dishon-Berkovits, M, & Koslowsky, M 2002, 'Determinants of Employee Punctuality', Journal Of Social Psychology, 142, 6, pp. 723-739.

Drapp, B. (1998) 'Strikers sought respect, dignity from McDonald's, Cleveland Plain Dealer , 13 May: 1E.

Ervin P. J., & Iverson, R. D. (1994). Strategies in absence management, Asia Pasific Journal of Human Resources

'Fast Food Nation: The Dark Side of the All-American Meal (Book)' 2004, California Journal, 35, 8, pp. 42-43, Academic Search Complete, EBSCOhost, viewed 10 August 2013.

'Fast Food Restaurants Industry (NAICS 72221)' 2013, United States Fast Food Restaurants Industry Capital & Expenses Report, pp. 1-218, Business Source Complete, EBSCOhost, viewed 9 August 2013.

Fujino Y, Mizoue T, Izumi H, Kumashiro M, Hasegawa T, Yoshimura T. 2001. Job stress and mental health among permanent night workers. J Occup Health. 43:301–306.

Groeneveld, J., & Shaizn, M. (1985). The effect of corrective interviews with alcohol dependent employees: A study of 37 supervisor–subordinate dyads. Employee Assistance Quarterly, 1,3–73.

Grunert, K.G. (2005). Food quality and safety: Consumer perception and demand. European Review of Agricultural Economics, 32(3), 369-391

Gupta, N., & Jenkins, G. D. (1983). Tardiness as a manifestation of employee withdrawal. Journal of Business Research, 11, 61–75.

Horowitz TS, Tanigawa T. 2002. Circadian-based new technologies for night workers. Ind Health.40:223–236.

Hanisch, K. A., & Hulin, C. L. (1990). Job attitudes and organizational withdrawal: An examination of retirement and other voluntary withdrawal behaviors. Journal of Vocational Behavior

Iverson, R.D., Olekalns, M., & Erwin, P.J. (1998). Affectively, organizational stressors and absenteesm: A causal model of burnout and its consequences.

Jamal, M. (1984). Job stress and job performance controversy: An empirical assessment. Organizational Behavior and Human Performance, 33,1–21

Johns, G. (1997). Contemporary research on absence from work: Correlates, causes, and consequenses. In C. L. Cooper & I.T. Robertson

Johns, G., & Nicholson, N. (1982). The meaning of absence: New strategies for theory and research. Research in Organizational Behavior, 4,127–173

Kalman, F. (2012). Super-Sized Learning: McDonald's Chris Lyons. (cover story). Chief Learning Officer, 11(10), 22-25.

Kearney J. Food consumption trends and drivers. Philos Trans R Soc Lond B Biol Sci. 2010;365:2793–2807.

Koslowsky, M. (1987). Antecedents and consequences of turnover: An integrated systems approach. Genetic, Social and General Psychology Monographs, 113, 271-292.

Koslowsky, M., Sagie, A., Krausz, M., & Singer, A. D. (1997). Correlates of employee lateness: Some theoretical considerations, Journal of applied psychology.

14

Landy F. J., Rastegary, H., Thayer J., & Colvin, C. (1991). Time urgency: The construct and its measurement. Journal of Applied Psychology, 76,644–657.

Leidner, R. (1993c) Fast Food, Fast Talk: Service Work and the Routinization of Everyday Life , Berkeley, CA: University of California Press.

Leigh, J. P., & Lust, J. (1988). Determinations of employee tardiness. Work and Occupations, 15,78–95.

Muesser, R. E. (1953). The weather and other factors influencing employee punctuality. Journal of Applied Psychology, 37,329–338

Naska A, Fouskakis D, Oikonomou E, et al. Dietary patterns and their sociodemographic determinants in 10 European countries: data from the DAFNE databank. Eur J Clin Nutr. 2006;60:181–190

Nicholson, N. (1977). Absence behavior and attendance motivation: A conceptual synthesis. Journal of Management Studies, 14,152–231.

Pati AK, Chandrawanshi A. 2001. Assessment of anxiety level and mental health status in spouses and children of day-working and shift-working men. Biol Rhythm Res. 32:45–59.

Price, J. L. & Mueller, C. W. (1986). Absenteeism and turnover of hospital employees

Punctuality Counts 2006, T+D, 60, 7, p. 11, Academic Search Complete, EBSCOhost, viewed 23 August 2013.

Röhr, A., Lu'ddecke, A., Drusch, S., Muller, M.J. & Alvensleben, R.V. (2005). Food quality and safety – Consumer perception and public health concern. Food Control, 16, 649-655.

Royle, T 2002, 'Labour Relations in the Global Fast Food Industry (Book)', Employee Relations, 24, 5, pp. 561-563

Rydell SA. Why Eat at Fast-Food Restaurants: Reported Reasons among Frequent Consumers. J Am Diet Assoc. 2008;108(12):2066-70.

Schlosser, E. (2001), Fast Food Nation, Houghton Mifflin, New York, NY.

Shafritz, J. M. (1980). Dictionary of personnel management and labor relations. Oak Park, IL: Moore.

Shapira, Z., & Griffith, T. L. (1990). Comparing the work values of engineers with managers, production, and clerical workers: A multivariate analysis. Journal of Organizational Behavior, 11, 281–292.

Steers, R.M., & Rhodes, S.R (1984). Knowledge and speculation about absenteeism. In P.S. Goodman & R.S. Atkin (Eds.),Absenteeism: New approaches to understanding, measuring, and managing employee absence(pp. 229–275). San Francisco: Jossey-Bass.

Suzuki K, Ohida T, Kaneita Y, Yokoyama E, Miyake T, Harano S, Yagi Y, Ibuka E, Kaneko A,Tsutsui T, Uchiyama M. 2004. Mental health status, shift work, and occupational accidents among hospital nurses in Japan. J Occup Health. 46:448–454.

Tannock, S. (2001) Youth at Work: The Unionized Fast-food and Grocery Workplace, Philadelphia: Temple University Press.

Van Giezen, Robert W. 1994, Occupational Wages in the Fast-Food Restaurant Industry

15